A. C. PING has traveled extensively and
lived and worked in the United Kingdom,
Africa, and Australia.

He has been many things, including
a futures trader, limo driver, teacher, scuba
divemaster, tour guide, and
corporate consultant.

Now he writes about new ways
of living and working and assists
individuals and organizations in making
their bold visions become reality.

A. C. Ping

MARLOWE & COMPANY
NEW YORK

Published by
Marlowe & Company
An Imprint of Avalon Publishing Group Incorporated
245 West 17th Street · 11th Floor
New York, NY 10011-5300

AVALON
publishing group incorporated

First published by Ricochet Productions in Australia in 2001.
Previously published by Penguin Books Australia Ltd. in Australia
in 2003.

Library of Congress Cataloging-in-Publication Data
Ping, A.C., 1965–
Do / A.C. Ping.
p. cm.
Originally oublished: Australia : Penguin Books Australia, 2003
ISBN 1-56924-421-9
1. Success—Religious aspects. I. Title.

BL65.S84.P56 2005
158—dc22
2004061009

9 8 7 6 5 4 3 2 1

Designed by Pauline Neuwirth, Neuwirth & Associates, Inc.

Printed in Canada

for izzie

acknowledgments

Wow! What can I say?
Except that I feel so blessed by the love
and support of so many fantastic people.
First, I really want to thank all of the people who read *BE*
and then took the time to write, e-mail, or speak to me
about it. The inspiration for this book came from
that interaction and the request to "continue the
conversation." I'm also grateful to all of the people
who allowed me to bounce ideas off them,
especially the younger people by whom I was often
reminded that you don't have to be old to be wise.

This book wouldn't be what it is without a slice of
African energy. I'm indebted to Fi for letting me share
her little hideaway and to my other friends in
the Drakensberg—Sofi, Kirsten, Keith, Mabutu,
Basil, Jane, and the rest of my extended "family."

I also want to thank all of the people who read the
initial drafts and gave me invaluable feedback—
Deborah, Tracy, Janine, Jonathan, Lotus, Mark,
and Chrissie. Thanks for your honesty, ideas, and
thoughtfulness. I really appreciate the time you spent
helping to get this book to its final stage.

Last, but certainly not least, I want to acknowledge
and thank my friend and editor Ruth and all of the people
at Penguin Australia, especially Ali and Anne. I hope this
heralds the beginning of a long and successful
relationship; I'm emboldened by your belief
and inspired by the future possibilities.

A. C. Ping

contents

Introduction   xvi

DO YOU   1

The authentic being   3
Put your ass on the line   8
The one who always knows   14
Playing with possibilities   19
Seeing if the future fits   25
Set your intention   30
Pray rain   33
Gathering courage   35
The spiritual warrior   46
Paradigm inertia   51
Strategic intent   54
The power of patience and persistence   57
Moments loaded with destiny   59
The pillars   63

DO HAPPY   67

  Where from?   69

  Hozho   72

  Be the source   75

  Captain Karma and the dharma police   78

  Bulletproof positive attitude   83

  Don't blink!   85

  Don't fight the world   91

  Stop, think, then act!   94

  I believe, you believe, we disagree!   96

  Stay in the conversation   102

  Learning to fly   106

  Gratitude takes you to joy   108

  Here's to the problems of freedom!   110

DO ONE   113

  The rational fool   115

  The big puzzle   119

  Freedom reigns in truth   122

  The light at the edge of the world   125

  Faith and expectation   127

  I to we   130

  Judgement locks the gate to possibility 133

  The true impact of unity   135

  Putting it all together   137

  The meaning of life   141

introduction

No, try not! Do or do not! There is no try.
—YODA, *The Empire Strikes Back*

it is one of the classic scenes from the movie *The Empire Strikes Back*: on some far away planet, Yoda is balanced on Luke's foot while Luke balances on one hand, simultaneously using the force to levitate rocks. Suddenly, Luke's spaceship sinks into the swamp and Luke loses his concentration, which sends Yoda tumbling to the ground.

"I'll never get it out of there," says Luke.

"Use the force," Yoda replies.

"I'll try," answers Luke, to which Yoda responds angrily with the quote above.

Wouldn't it be great to have your own personal Yoda? To have a mentor, someone to call upon in moments of crisis

and uncertainty? He'd certainly make a fun dinner guest . . . "Yoda, can you pass the salt? And by the way, how do we solve the Middle East crisis? And what exactly IS the meaning of life?"

Certainty. It is what we all seek in our lives. Crises and chaos surround us and cause great anxiety. If only we could have certainty, someone or something we could call on to answer the vexing questions of life . . . *Will this relationship work out? Is this the right job to take? Should I move to a new place?*

But nothing is certain, everything changes, and the only way to find answers is to DO. But "doing" means taking risks, dipping our toes in the water of life, making waves, sometimes getting it right, sometimes wrong, upsetting people, challenging ourselves, challenging others . . .

There are plenty of answers out there. Just look around your local bookstore and you'll see offers on how to achieve happiness, fulfilment, relationship success, and material success. But always, as Yoda says, the trick is in the doing.

That is why this book is not about the why but about the how. How do you put some of these concepts to work at changing your life so you can be happy and fulfilled? This book is the follow-up to my book *BE*, and although it can be read on its own, it will make more sense after reading *BE*. *DO* is divided into three parts—**DO YOU**, **DO HAPPY**, and **DO ONE**. The central premise is that first you must

be able to find you, then you can act on this discovery to be happy, and finally, with happiness, comes the abundance to transcend the self and be one.

Like *BE*, this is a collection of ideas and concepts that have helped me on my journey. Like *BE*, it is about sharing these ideas in the hope that some or all of them may help you on your journey. *BE* was about encouraging you to think; now this book is about making you DO. So, let us begin . . .

DO You

the authentic being

One should not avoid one's tests, although they
are perhaps the most dangerous game one could
play and are in the end tests which are taken before
ourselves and before no other judge.
—*Beyond Good and Evil*, NIETZSCHE

you must be yourself, find the real you and live the
life you were put on this world to live . . ." I've heard that again
and again. Hmmmm . . . Excuse my ignorance, but what the
hell does that mean exactly? And I do mean EXACTLY. Please,
no more waffly, waffly talk. Just tell me how to make sense
of it and how to do something about it.

Have you ever felt this way, maybe while sitting in some
sort of spiritual-growth, self-helpy type of meeting? As everyone around you smiles dreamily and exudes love, crapping

on about how their life has just changed so completely, you're sitting there thinking, *What's the big deal?*

I have . . . And yes, I know I'm a cynic but so are lots of people. So how does a cynic answer the question, *Who am I?*

I believe it's all about authenticity. If we are put on this world for a reason and if we have certain things to accomplish while we are here, then there is a certain way of living life that will fulfil this purpose. Authenticity is about finding the real you so you can live as the genuine article rather than as a cheap fake. So you can form genuine relationships and stand on a strong foundation that enables you to live your life with authority. Without a strong foundation you will simply flop from one thing to the next, plodding along until your time here is up.

So what is the Authentic Being?

the three domains of life

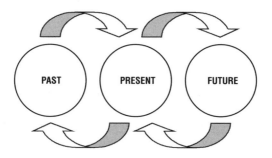

DO

This is the way of looking at the world that was introduced in *BE*. We can divide the world (and our lives) into three domains—the Past, the Present, and the Future.

In the Past we have all the experiences, opinions, judgments, and baggage that we've accumulated during our lives. Collectively, this forms our fixed view of the world and provides the basis for our understanding of, and interaction with, the world around us. If we simply mark out our territory and stay firmly fixed in the Past, we will never create anything new. When faced with every new situation we simply look back to what happened in the Past and make decisions based on those experiences. This, in turn, perpetuates the views of the Past in the Present. For example, if we see the world as a dangerous place where everyone is trying to deceive us, then we will never risk allowing people to get close to us, which limits our opportunities of forming new relationships.

In the Present things either are or are not. Either you are sitting here right now reading this book or you are not—no debate, is or isn't. The Present is where things happen; it's the only place where spirit and matter meet, which means it is your opportunity to influence the material world.

The Future is a blank canvas where anything is possible. It's where you can dream your dreams and create infinite possibilities. It's the place where Vision and Ideals reside. However, on it's own the Future is just like the Past—a talk fest. It's where you dream. The only place to DO is in the present.

DO

So, what's this got to do with authenticity?

Well, the Authentic Being is the one who takes possession of their possibilities of being. Sound too lofty? Okay, try this—the Authentic Being takes possession of and responsibility for future-based ideals such as values, vision, and dreams and then DOES SOMETHING ABOUT IT. Get it?

Try looking at it graphically.

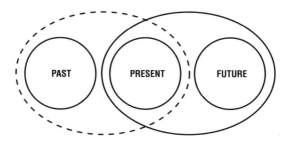

The Authentic Being is the one who lives their life within the solid oval which possesses their Present and their Future possibilities. The inauthentic being is the one who lives their life within the dashed oval on the left, where their future possibilities have been relinquished or suppressed. If you're in the right-hand oval then you actively identify and pursue your dreams, vision, and ideals. If you're in the left-hand loop then you are focused on the Past, have given up the possibility of fulfilling your dreams, and essentially decided to mark out your territory and maintain your station.

I believe that all of us begin life in the right-hand oval but somewhere along life's path we discover that it is difficult to strive for our dreams. So we make a whole lot of compromises and then settle for what we get. Our dreams rot within us and over time manifest as bitterness. We become the person who always has reasons for why things aren't possible rather than why things are. We are filled with regret. We effectively shut down and spend our time justifying the position we have taken in life. If someone comes to us with outrageous dreams, we are the first to shoot them down and tell them why they are not possible. "Get back in your box," we say. "Don't be so ridiculous."

Is that you? Have you become the person who says things like, "Life's a chore, you can't always get what you want"?

Since you're reading this book, maybe you're sick of the way you are being. Has something happened that's pissed you off enough to make you want to change?

Let's try it out. How do you find the authentic you? How do you take possession of the possibilities of your being?

Put your ass
on the line

Wayfarer there is no way
We make the way by walking.
—MACHADO, Spanish poet

I hope you didn't think this would be easy, that there would be a simple answer, an amazing revelation that would instantly transform you into the person you've always wanted to be. Have you been going from course to course, seminar to seminar, book to book, looking for THE elusive solution? If only we could find Yoda or some other guru to help us stop farting about and just give us all the answers then it would be a piece of cake . . . But life's not like that—we have to do the work ourselves.

So, how committed are you? That's the first question you need to ask. Commitment means being willing to hammer

a stake into the ground and take a stand by it until it becomes reality. But you have to have leverage. Without leverage you will get nowhere. Leverage allows you to multiply your efforts for maximum effect. It's difficult to lift a bag of cement off the ground. But if you get a plank, place it over a block, roll the bag onto one end, and then stand on the other end, you'll find it's easy.

Consider this example. I used to work for a management consultancy that focused on training people in leadership and change management. Now the guy who ran the company was pretty smart and every time a client came to him with a request for training and raised the inevitable question of cost, he'd answer $60K. It didn't matter if it was for a five-day training course or for a month's retainer fee, the answer was always $60K. Eventually we became so used to his answer that we started calling him the $60K man. One day I asked him about this and his reply opened my eyes. He said, "There must be something at stake, otherwise there is no leverage and only a limited possibility for change."

"What does that mean?" I asked.

"How much more seriously does the client take our work when they pay so much money for it? Imagine if we only charged them $100—they would come to the training, listen to it for interest, but then most likely go back to work and just keep doing things the way they've always done them. The money is just a way of gaining leverage, that's all."

It's the same with your life. If you have nothing at stake

and you only half-heartedly commit to changing then it will only be a project driven by whim. You'll go through the motions, waiting for something to happen to provide you with evidence that change is worthwhile. Then maybe, just maybe, you will make more of a commitment, but not until you have the evidence . . .

So, how do you find the leverage and the commitment to change?

Are you unhappy enough with your current reality that you are willing to risk who you are now to create the new you? Are you ready to say goodbye to the victim within you? It's easy to read about things or listen to others but it's much harder to do. So take some time now and consciously decide whether or not you want to change. Make a list. Why do you want to change? What's so wrong with the way you are now that you wish to be different?

Why I want to change . . .

_____

_____

_____

_____

_____

_____

Parts of me I want to let go . . .

_____

_____

_____

_____

_____

_____

NOTES

My commitment to change is . . .

_____

_____

_____

_____

_____

_____

_____

NOTES

DO

Without a degree of tension in your life there will be no motivation to do the hard yards that are required for change. You need to be able to answer the question, *What's in it for you?* Otherwise it is easy just to slip back into the old way of doing things when it all gets too hard.

So now you should have a list of reasons why you want to change. If not, stop reading NOW and do it—go on. If you keep reading now without having listed your reasons, guess what? You're not serious about it . . .

Now you have your list. So what's your commitment? How much time are you willing to spend to make this happen? One hour per week, one hour per day, what? Be serious about it and think it through, realistically. If you have only three hours per week then commit to three hours per week, not six. Don't make a noose for yourself.

Now, at the bottom of your list of reasons for why you want to change, write: *My commitment to change is x hours per week and I will continue to spend x hours per week until my goal is reached*.

Now that you're committed, let's see what's next.

the one who always knows

True genius is saying what is in your heart,
because it is in everyone's heart.
—*Self Reliance*, RALPH WALDO EMERSON

why is it that we can read books like this and say to ourselves, "Hmmm, that makes perfect sense, but somewhere deep down I knew that already"? I think we all have a little part of us that already does know this stuff. The fundamental teaching of the Essenes, an ancient people from the Middle Eastern region, is that we are already healed. It's just a matter of getting in touch with that part of ourselves. And that's the trick—if you are going to find the real you, the authentic you, then you need to find a level of awareness that allows you to truly see yourself. If you can do that, then you are in a position to be truthful with yourself.

So, once again, how do you do it?

In *BE* we talked about the need to stop reacting to things and to find some space where you can listen to yourself. We talked about the benefits of meditation and that's really where all of this starts. You need to find a way of nurturing the observer.

Let's try an example. Recently I was talking to a friend of mine about all this stuff. Right away he said, "Oh, yeah, I know what you're talking about. Just a little while ago I was getting in the car to go to work and I had this distinct feeling that I needed to contact my ex-girlfriend, that she wanted to see me desperately."

"And did you?" I asked.

"No, but I found out later that at exactly the same time she was sitting at home wondering where I was and really needed me."

"So why didn't you call her at the time?"

"I didn't think it was the right thing to do. I felt like calling but we'd only just separated so I ignored the feeling."

Why don't we act on the advice from that little voice inside our heads who butts into our lives from time to time? I believe it is because we are so used to accepting the validity of what we can see and touch that sometimes we don't acknowledge how we feel. Then a feeling like that arises and it is out of sync with our rational or logical way of looking at the world, so we dismiss it. And the more we dismiss our feelings or intuitions the weaker they become. It's like the

little kid who constantly asks for our attention. If we ignore them often enough then slowly we tune them out and eventually we just can't hear them.

How often have you been about to do something when a little voice inside your head suggests an alternative action, which is not supported by the evidence in front of you? How often have you ignored that voice and later, when things have fallen apart, reflected and thought, *Damn! If only I'd listened*.

Relationships are a classic example of this. You meet someone new who you think is quite nice and even though a nagging thought inside your brain says, "No, forget it," you proceed anyway. Then, because the relationship is nice, not mind-blowing, but just nice, you stay in it. But the longer you stay in it the more the nag continues and the more you have to dredge to find logical reasons for remaining. And the longer you stay in it, the more habitual it gets and the harder it is to get out. Sometimes along the way, as if you are being taunted, you even get introduced to someone, usually one of your partner's best friends, and straight away you know that this is EXACTLY the person you are looking for. But of course you can do nothing! Then finally you do pluck up the nerve to get out, often using some feeble premise after many trivial arguments—like whose turn it is to do the dishes. The other party stares at you in disbelief as if to say, "But things have been going along so nicely." And, yes, that's just it—nice isn't good enough . . . But I digress.

It's easy to brush over intuitive feelings because that's not how we are taught to make decisions. Scientific method and logic decrees that one must examine the available evidence, THEN make an appropriate decision—not take a quiet moment, tap into how you really feel about something, then make a decision.

So, doing it . . .

Begin by taking some time just before you go to sleep at night to reflect on the day's events. How did you really FEEL about everything that happened? Is there anything you did, or are there decisions you made, that you are unhappy about? If so, resolve to do something about them. Then start doing the same thing in the morning. Think about the day to come and whether or not you have any strong feelings about what you are about to do or the decisions you will have to make.

Next, you have to get out of the cycle of rush-rush-rush, time-is-money thinking. Bad decisions will haunt you for a lot longer than the time you may lose through delaying decisions. These days everyone pushes and many people are quick to suggest there is something wrong with you if you take a long time to make up your mind. Pressure, pressure, pressure, come on, hurry up for Christ's sake, the clock is ticking . . . Just tell such a person to back off, it's YOUR life, no one can take responsibility for it but you. They won't be the ones paying for it if you make bad decisions, so don't let them push you.

The good news is that the more often you take the time to check in with your little observer, the clearer the message will become and the quicker you will be able to make decisions. BUT, and this is a big BUT, the reprogramming takes time, so be patient.

The more you stop the chaos around you and listen in, the better you will get at it and the more connected you will be with your feelings. Remember though, this is just like going to the gym. The first time you go, you have to force yourself. Everything is unfamiliar, you don't know how to use the equipment, you hurt afterward and you can't lift much weight. But when you go regularly you get into the habit, you know exactly how to use the equipment, you lift larger weights and you feel charged up afterward.

> As you go the way of life, you will see a great chasm.
> Jump! It is not as wide as you think.
> —Native American saying

The first step to meditation and tapping into the real you is taking the first step. Remember your commitment? Well, it's here that it begins. You don't have to take an hour every day. To start, you just need to start. Just five minutes lying in bed before you go to sleep or before you get out of bed will start you on the journey. From there it is up to you, but as soon as you see the benefits you will be inspired to do more. Oh, and remember, be patient!

playing with possibilities

Dreams are visions
from which reality is made
so keep on dreaming.
—ANON

in *BE* we talked about the whole Vision thing. Hopefully now you can see that it all fits into the idea of being authentic. You need to have clarity of Vision before you can take ownership of it.

I talk with many people about Vision, the elusive answer to "What do you REALLY want?" It's incredible how many people have absolutely no idea and manage to torture themselves on a regular basis because they don't know. How about you? Have you got it down pat or are you struggling along with what you have, trying from time to time—

in between rushing from work to the gym, to drinks with friends, to home and back again—to find a chance to have a really good think about it?

Do you do brainstorming at work? Or have you ever done a creative thinking class? Do you draw or paint? Well, try it out on your life. You have a time commitment so allocate some to brainstorming your life. You could even invite some close friends over for a dinner party, have a few drinks, and do your brainstorming then if you think it will help. No, I'm not kidding, really! I mean, why the hell not? It seems to me where most people struggle is in the generation of possibilities. Our world tends to lock us into a certain way of living. Before we know it our view of the world becomes very narrow and we can't see beyond it. This is one of the reasons I like to travel. There's something very mind-expanding about spending time with people from different cultures. Put it this way—when I was working in the United Kingdom as a management consultant, it seemed very important that we all drove nice cars, wore expensive clothes, ate at good restaurants, and lived in comfortable houses. There were two defining concerns in that environment: how my career was going, and how I could make more money so I could buy a better car and live in a better house. If I was unhappy, the simple solution, as encouraged by our free-market capitalist society, was to get a different job. I was on a production line that would have deposited me at the other end with a large

retirement fund and a big tick from society in the "success" box, but still no idea what I REALLY wanted to do.

Then I got to Africa. I found myself clutching grimly to a horse that had a hard old saddle that did its best to rub through my skin as we made our way up the side of a mountain to visit a small village where food was scarce and the water from the well was barely drinkable. When we arrived, no one asked me what I did for a living, no one asked me what sort of car I drove or how much money I made. They only wanted to know who I was, as defined by my beliefs, not what I was as defined by my possessions. I had nothing to hide, and not once did I think about my career or my car. I met people who were incredibly happy and engaged with them at a very deep level. It made me realize that there is more than one way to live and that to think otherwise is to blind oneself to limitless possibilities.

So, if you struggle with generating possibilities take any help you can get to knock you out of your comfort zone. They are only ideas, and it is fun to play.

Try these out for starters. Where do you want to live? In a city, in the country, by the mountains, by the sea, in a forest, in a desert, in the snow, in a house, in an apartment, in a yurt? What sort of human interaction do you want to have? None; just a few close friends who only come round by invitation for quiet dinner parties; heaps of people who drop by uninvited and challenge you about everything while getting blind drunk on YOUR red wine;

family who come by to drop off their kids for you to babysit so they can go shopping or see a secret admirer? What sort of work do you want to do? Inside or outside, corporate or community, physical or intellectual? How much money do you want to make? None—grow veggies and live by bartering the sweaters you knit from the alpacas you have grazing on your little plot of land; some—just enough to pay for the paint you use to paint the sweeping, panoramic views from your cliff-top home; enough—so you can send the kids to a nice school and buy yourself new clothes from time to time; lots—so you can buy a new Ferrari that you'll park in the front drive of your three-story house so the neighbors can see it and turn green with envy?

Is this all just tooooo silly for you? Well maybe it is silly, but do you see the point? Play around with it, don't be limited to what you have right now or by what other people think you should be doing. THEN when you have a good idea of where you want to live, work, and how you want to interact, ask yourself "What type of person do I want to be?" Extrovert, introvert, friendly, gregarious? And "Which do I believe are the most important values and principles in life?" The exercises in *BE* will help you to answer these questions.

Now you have to try this on for size.

My ideal place to live is . . .

_____

_____

_____

_____

I'll support myself by . . .

_____

_____

_____

_____

The type of human interaction
I'll have is . . .

_____

_____

_____

_____

I'll be the type of person who is . . .

_____

_____

_____

_____

NOTES

seeing if the
future fits

Those who dream by night in the dusty recesses of their
minds wake in the day to find that all was vanity; but the
dreamers of the day are dangerous men, for they may act
their dreams with open eyes, and make it possible.
—T. E. LAWRENCE (Lawrence of Arabia)

have you ever seen a television commercial
for a new style of clothing and thought, *Wow, gotta have one
of those?* Did you gather your credit cards together and
rush into the shop, only to find when you tried it on that
while it looked great on the model it looked like a potato
sack on you? Hmmm . . . Okay, the same thing can happen
here. Except it's hard to go and try on a new you.

But there is another way. Visualization meditation.

When you have narrowed down the possibilities and you

have a grand vision of the new you, you need to see if the vision fits. So, take yourself off to a quiet space, to somewhere you will not be interrupted and do a little daydreaming. Apparently Edison used to go snook fishing but never put any bait on his hook—in snook country you never interrupted someone who was fishing.

Anyway, sit down quietly, close your eyes, and visualize the ideal life you have planned for yourself. See it, smell it, touch it, listen to it. . . . How does it fit? Is it exciting? Does it feel comfortable? If not, what's nagging you about it? What SCARES you about it?

Yes, stop there for a second. What is it that scares you about it? Do you get a weird tightening in the stomach when you visualize your ideal life? One that makes you feel like you can't breathe properly? Is it a kind of anxious feeling that you can't quite put your finger on?

You need to work out what this feeling is. If something is hindering your comfort you need to identify it or you will subconsciously self-sabotage. So, go back to sitting quietly visualizing your ideal life. Now when that feeling surfaces don't react to it. Concentrate on your breathing, focus on being relaxed, and don't push the feeling away. Instead, let it rise up. Allow it to reveal itself as an image or as a clear and specific feeling. This may take some time and several attempts but you must persist. When you have identified the fear, write it down. We will come back and deal with it in a moment.

I remember conducting this exercise with a group of people who were setting up small businesses. One young woman was planning a business that put nannies in touch with overseas clients and she already had many people interested. But after doing this exercise she came to me in a distraught state.

"I can't do this," she said.

"Why not?"

"Well, when I visualized my successful business, I realised that the thing that was missing was children. I really want to have children."

We talked it through and it turned out that all she had to do was structure the business slightly differently to allow for the possibility of having children. But she wouldn't have known that unless she'd tried it on. Most likely she would have gone through all the work of setting up the business and making it successful only to find that it trapped her into a way of being that didn't make her happy.

So take the time, play with the vision and make adjustments if it doesn't fit. Ill-fitting lives are much harder to fix than ill-fitting clothing.

Next, take it to a deeper level. Try the ideal day exercise.

Determine what your ideal day in your ideal world looks like, from the moment you wake up until the moment you go to sleep. When you open your eyes, what do you see? What do you feel? What's the first thing you do? And then what? During the day, what things do you do? Where do you go?

How do you get there? Who's there when you get there? When you get home, what's the first thing you do? What gives you joy?

These two exercises are critical in being able to create the life you want. Without a clear idea of what you want you will only be reactive. Things that seem like a good idea will most likely turn out to be just that—a good idea and nothing more. If you know exactly what you want then you have a better chance of getting it.

My ideal day . . .

_____

_____

_____

_____

_____

_____

_____

_____

_____

_____

_____

_____

_____

_____

_____

NOTES

set your intention

We are what we think.
All that we are arises from our thoughts.
Within our thoughts we make our world.
—BUDDHA

what do you do with this vision now? Sit back and wait for it to arrive? Cast it aside as a pipe dream? No, you need to charge it with energy, so the next ingredient is intention. You must intend for it to come into being, otherwise it will lay dormant as just another unfulfilled wish.

The word "intention" comes from the Latin "to stretch toward" and it is the inspiration for vision. Without intention vision is nothing. So, what exactly is intention?

Intention is the act of consciously putting energy into bringing something into being. The way the world works is

that like attracts like. So if you spend your whole time thinking that you always put yourself in losing situations, then guess what? You attract those situations to you. But if you think and act in a way that puts energy into the manifestation of your vision, then you will bring that vision into being.

Now, a word of caution here. It's not enough to work out what it is you don't want and then put energy into that. If you do, then you will attract what you don't want. Of course that reinforces to you that you don't want it and you put even more of a charge into it.

For example, a woman I know started having a string of boyfriends who turned out to be seeking a mother figure in their lives. Every new guy she met seemed fine on the surface but soon expected her to cook for him and to generally run his life. The man became a little boy and instead of being a woman she became a mother. The problem was that the more often this happened, the more often she said, "I don't want to be with another man who needs a mother."

But because she had a charge on that statement, she kept attracting those men, continuing the vicious cycle.

Are you in a cycle like this? Do you keep finding yourself in situations that you don't want? Do you find yourself thinking more about what you don't want than what you do want?

If the answer is yes, you've got to change your internal dialogue. Stop right now and write down a list of all of the things that you don't want and consciously think about. Once you have the list, you need to let those things go. Turn

them around into what you do want. One way of doing this that I love (and this is why there isn't a "Notes" page with this question on it) is to take the list and throw it into a fire. As the paper turns to smoke and disappears, consciously watch those things disappear from your life. Let them go and release the hold they had on you.

Be clear about what you do want and then consciously put energy into it. Spend time every morning when you meditate to set your intention of what you want and who you want to be.

pray rain

it took me a long time to figure this bit out. I always wondered why some people had no trouble at all manifesting their dreams while others kept struggling, despite all their good intentions.

In a word the answer is BELIEF!

You can have the best and clearest intentions in the world but if you have no belief you are nowhere. If you want to see it in equation form then INTENTION + BELIEF = CREATION.

You must believe in the manifestation of your dreams. But what you need is not just any sort of belief. This belief is crystal clear and without doubt absolutely certain in the inevitability of the outcome.

Try this. There is a story about a guy who went to Arizona to visit his Native American friend. The region had been suffering from a terrible drought, so the Native American asked his friend to join him in a trek up into the mountains to a sacred medicine wheel. They treked all day and finally reached the medicine wheel as the sun was setting. The white guy was full of excitement, expecting his friend to perform some amazing ritual. The man sat down for a while, gathered his thoughts, then entered the medicine wheel and danced slowly around it with his eyes closed. After a few minutes he finished dancing and returned to his friend to say they could go.

"So, did you pray for rain?" the white guy asked.

The man looked at him. "No, I saw myself dancing in the streets while the heavens opened, felt the raindrops on my face, saw the puddles forming, and felt the joy that everyone experienced. If I had prayed for rain then rain would never come."

Do you see the difference? You need to put energy into the ACTUAL vision and draw it into this world, NOT into hoping for something to happen—then it is just a wish.

The other thing you need to do is SEE YOURSELF IN THE PICTURE. It's no use visualizing the ideal situation you want without seeing yourself in it. Guess what happens then? Yep! You manifest the situation, but you are only an observer.

Belief puts the charge on the intention and the intention inspires the vision. By having clarity of vision, clear intention, and belief you CAN create what you want in the world. Aligning all three is the key.

gathering courage

Life shrinks or expands
in proportion to one's courage
—ANAÏS NIN

ah! Courage, yes, what is it? How do you find it? Why do some people have more than others?

How about this—if you had no fear, would you have courage? I think so. If I had no fear of jumping from a hundred-foot cliff into the sea then I'd just go ahead and do it—wouldn't even think twice, pah, just jump, no big deal . . . But someone with no fear is downright dangerous. I'm sure you know people like that. They're the ones who end up getting you into trouble by dragging you into some mad scheme which usually involves breaking the law in some way and they have no fear of the consequences.

Our fears are useful. They stop us from doing things that might cause us harm, so surely they aren't bad things. I think courage is about acknowledging your fears but not letting them dictate your actions. The key is to work out which fears are useful to you and which ones aren't. So how the hell do you do that?

Well, some are easy, like the fear that stops you from walking out in front of a bus—definitely a no-brainer! Even though I've never been hit by a bus I know it's not a good thing to do . . .

Recently I went with a friend to a beach in Australia where there is an amazing rockpool. It is sheltered from the sea on one side by a reef and on the other side there is a huge, craggy rock you can climb up. When we arrived we saw young kids climbing the rock and leaping off the top into the rockpool. Now it is not a small rock, probably forty feet high, so that's quite a leap. The kids were having lots of fun and it seemed like a great thing to do. When they'd finished their fun, the first thing I did was jump into the pool to check how deep it was and if there were any concealed rocks just below the surface. No problem, the pool was at least twenty feet deep with a clear, sandy bottom. As long as you jumped out into the middle there really wasn't a great chance of doing yourself a major injury.

We climbed the rock but once we were at the top it was a long, long way down! Even though we'd seen the kids jump and

get out safely and we knew the pool was deep and we knew there were no hidden rocks, we were still afraid. Why? Well, suddenly our minds were full of "what ifs?" What if we slipped and landed on the edge and broke our necks? What if there was a hidden rock that we hadn't seen? What if the kids didn't hit the bottom because they were only small but people our size would plummet straight down and break both legs? What if? What if? What if? Shit! We were paralyzed by fear. Even though the evidence said "Jump," our fears said "No way!"

What to do? When faced with this sort of situation you need to ask that critical question—*What do you want?* Well damn it, I wanted to have as much fun as those kids had so I stopped thinking about it and just jumped! Yeeeeeee haaaaaa! Splash, no broken bones and what a rush!

"Come on!" I yelled to my friend.

"No way!" he yelled back. "I'm not doing that!" He climbed down from the rock, then jumped into the pool. He was pissed off, damaged ego and all . . .

"Hey, come on, it's not that far," I said.

"Yeah, but once you get up there it's a really long way down!"

"Oh, come on, look at it! It's not that far!"

Sure enough, when we looked up at the rock from the pool it didn't look far at all. The problem was that once you were at the top the distance seemed magnified. My friend really wanted to jump and of course I wasn't going to let him

off the hook. He knew that if we went home and he hadn't jumped then I would rib him about it for quite a while.

"Just don't think about it," I said. "Just get up there and jump, don't hesitate!"

He thought about it for a while. Then, with a bit more nagging from me, eventually he climbed the rock, barely even glanced over the edge and just jumped.

Have you been in a situation like this?

Our fears are based on our past experiences—so we have firsthand evidence—or on things that other people have told us or that we have learned—so we have second-hand evidence—or, and this is the tricky one, stories that we have inside our heads that come from god-knows-where. Each of these fears can be magnified tenfold, or maybe even a thousandfold, by the what ifs. Some of our fears may even arise from a combination of all of these things!

This is the key question you need to ask: *Does fear stop you from doing what you want to do?* Remember, fear never bites as hard as regret. If you REALLY want to do something then you need to face the fear, otherwise you will reach the stage where you are just full of regrets. Know what I mean? You become the person who always says, "I wish I'd done that." Or you listen to other people's stories and wish they were about you. Authenticity, that's what it's all about, finding the courage to pursue your dreams. You may not achieve them but at least you know you tried and you will have no lingering regrets.

So, after the visioning exercise you should have a good idea of what it is you want to do and you can identify the fears that are in your way. You may have found that during your visualization meditation some of those fears reared their ugly heads and some of the stories were revealed.

Write a list of all these fears and then break them down into categories—fears that you have from past experience, fears that you have from secondhand experience, and fears that are based on your stories.

Look at them! You probably break out in a cold sweat just thinking about them! But all of these things stand between you and your dream so you need to deal with all of them.

So, let's go back to that Past, Present, and Future thing.

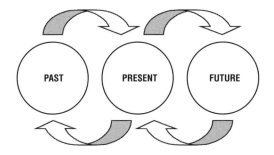

All of our fears are based in the Past domain. Our direct experiences are from the Past. What we heard from others was in the Past. If we have stories they are from the Past. The Future holds our vision and our dreams—there are no

fears there unless we project them forwards. So we need to take action in the Present to short-circuit those fears that are traveling toward our Future.

You must be the Gatekeeper. Between the Past and the Future is a bridge. Imagine that you have a sack on your back that holds all the things you've collected over the years of toil along the journey. It's very heavy. So heavy that it weighs you down, is hard to carry and is very unwieldy. Sometimes you even lose control of it as you pass other people on the path and it smacks into them and knocks them over. You know the sack is too heavy for you but you've been collecting these things for years and you really don't want to let any of them go. You'd rather clutch onto them and struggle than face the pain of letting them go.

Now you have climbed very high into the mountains and you come to a ravine that is so deep you can't even see the bottom. Up ahead is a narrow rope bridge. Your sack won't fit between the ropes on each side. You have a choice. Either stay with your things and look longingly toward the other side or, heaven forbid, go through the sack and leave some things behind.

Be the Gatekeeper. When you get to a bridge, and there are many along the path, don't mindlessly drag your baggage to the other side. Stop. Take the time to empty the bag. Work out what is useful and then leave the rest behind. You don't need it and it will only slow you down. But don't expect it to be easy. You've carried these things for a long

time so it will hurt to let them go. That is why you need to be clear about what you want and why you want it.

Step 1: If it's factual and you can do something about it, then do it!

What I mean by this is, well, let me give you an example.

I wanted to be able to speak confidently in public but even the thought of it used to send me into a cold sweat. I couldn't even raise my hand to ask a question in a seminar because I'd get so nervous that I would be unable to speak.

Anyway there I was, wanting to be able to speak in public but so ridiculously nervous that I just didn't know what to do. First step: I knew nothing about how to speak confidently in public so there was action I could take. I read books about public speaking and started learning more about the "tricks of the trade."

You may be in this position with some of your fears. If so, write down the things you need to do as a first step.

Step 2: Change your secondhand knowledge.

When I considered the idea of public speaking I knew that on a scale of fears most people rated it above dying! How ridiculous is that? But true! And the truth made me feel better because I thought to myself, *Well there's nothing wrong with me, I'm just like everybody else*. When I spoke to other people about it they'd reinforce this view too. They'd tell me how it terrified them and what a nightmare it was. So I

managed to gather a whole lot of evidence to support my view that public speaking was a terrifying thing to do. This in turn reinforced my fixed view of the world.

The problem was that I wanted to be able to speak in public so my fixed view of the world was stopping me from doing what I really wanted to do.

how to get out of it?

Decide what view you need to do what you want. Then start gathering evidence to support that view. I spoke to people who presented and asked them how they dealt with nervousness and how it felt to give a great presentation. Slowly but surely I gathered as much evidence to support the view that it was a fun thing to do as I had to support the view that it was a terrifying thing to do. Then every time I thought about it I started thinking more and more about the good stuff rather than the fear-based stuff.

Step 3: Change your story.

This is maybe the trickiest bit because it is all about reprogramming your brain. For a long time you've been telling yourself a story about how you can't do something because blah blah blah! Through the first two steps you have addressed some of the factual things and turned around the secondhand evidence, but the tricky bit is you.

back to my story . . .

So I'd read stuff about public speaking and I now had lots of evidence to show that it was a fun thing to do BUT I still had a negative story going round and round in my head—that public speaking terrified the living daylights out of me!

You know what happens when you listen to a song over and over again? You switch off the tape and the song keeps going in your head, around and around and around, and maybe you sing a bit to yourself which means you keep hearing it and keep reinforcing the song.

Same thing here. A little voice inside my head kept telling me over and over and over again: "You can't speak in public, you get really nervous and sweaty, lose your voice and make a total fool of yourself." Every time I thought about it I was terrified.

First try visualizing whatever the situation is. If you are like me you'll see the bad stuff straight away. When I started thinking about speaking in public the very first thing I saw was myself sweating! After that it was all downhill; my fears just piled up one on top of another. I could see myself sweating, then I saw myself shaking, then my voice was wavering, then I'd start having trouble with the overhead projector, then people would start asking me difficult questions, then I'd start feeling persecuted and finally I'd have painted myself into something like the Spanish Inquisition!

Does this happen to you? Do you throw your hands up in the air and say, "Stuff it, this is all too hard!"?

Let's try it again. This story has been going for a long time so it needs to be turned around slowly. The first step for me was seeing myself calm and relaxed instead of freaking out and sweating. For a long time that's all I did, just practiced visualizing myself calm and relaxed, nothing more.

Once I could comfortably see myself calm and relaxed I moved onto the next step, which was me speaking in a strong and clear voice. When I had that down pat I moved on. Finally I could sit down and visualize myself giving an entire presentation and see people clapping and congratulating me at the end of it.

Is this just mumbo jumbo? In a word, NO!

Recent advances in brain imaging technology show how this works scientifically. Researchers at the University of Pittsburgh and Carnegie Mellon[1] have shown that as people mentally prepare for a task they activate the prefrontal cortex—that part of the brain that performs executive functions and moves them into action. Without preparation the prefrontal cortex does not activate in advance. So the greater the prior activation, the better the person does at the task. The prefrontal cortex becomes particularly active

---

[1] "How the brain gets ready to perform," presentation at the 30th annual meeting of the Society of Neuroscience, New Orleans, November 2000, Cameron Carter, Angus McDonald, Stefan Ursu, Andy Stenger, Myeong Ho Sohn, and John Anderson.

when a person has to prepare to overcome a habitual response. The aroused prefrontal cortex marks the brain's focus on what's about to happen—without arousal the person will act out old, undesirable routines.

Makes sense, eh? Those old, undesirable routines are the fear-based habits that you have been practicing unconsciously for a very long time.

Obviously the final step is to actually do the act in question. However, since we are still looking at finding you and making the necessary preparations, we're going to leave this stuff for the moment and come back to it in the next part of this book.

Let's look at the battle with the self.

the spiritual warrior

The great epochs of our life are the occasions
when we gain the courage to rebaptise our
evil qualities as our best qualities.
—NIETZSCHE

it's relatively easy to fight others—you can see the enemy, focus on them, decide on a strategy and implement it. But the great battle, the battle of the Spiritual Warrior, is of the self versus the self.

There is a dark side in all of us. A side that we probably don't like very much, a side that harbors evil qualities such as envy, greed, and selfishness. Remember *Star Wars?* As Darth Vader fights with Luke he goads him: "Feel your anger, Luke, allow the dark side to take hold."

Hmmm . . . Ever feel like that? The genie comes out of the bottle and the rage overwhelms you. Or maybe it's jealousy? All you can feel is the power of the emotion and you become a slave to it—only to regret it later when you've calmed down.

Now you can choose what to do with this stuff. Either you deny that it is part of you and put lots of energy into keeping that little cork stuffed down into the bottle. Or you acknowledge that there is no duality in life, there is no separation, only the whole. Acknowledge your dark side and embrace it as part of who you are.

If you can do this you can begin the battle of the spiritual warrior. Our dark side is only the part of us where no light has yet penetrated. It is the part of us where we have the greatest opportunity for growth.

> It's easy for the impotent man to take a vow of
> chastity and for the poor to renounce wealth.
> —BUDDHA

So, how to begin? The trick is to be able to shine some light on this dark area of our selves. This is where the observer we have been nurturing becomes valuable.

We need to learn to stalk the self. Sound bizarre?

Remember, we are trying to find our true authentic selves so that we can embrace our lives and our future possibilities. If even one part of us is in denial then we can never

be truly whole. Remember also that as soon as we start reacting to things we lose our personal power: our power to create what we really want in a proactive way.

We can use our observer to stalk ourselves, to help gather our personal power, slowly but surely, and eventually we will have enough personal power to confront the worst aspects of our nature.

Look at it this way. Imagine you are stalking someone. (Not something I recommend by the way, but just imagine.) First, why are you stalking them? Well, because you want something. Second, what do you do? You follow them, watching their every move, gathering information about their habits and waiting for an opportunity to pounce.

It's the same thing with yourself. You stalk yourself because you want to confront, tame, and embrace your dark side. You do this by carefully observing your own habits and patterns and waiting for an opportunity to pounce.

Take anger as an example. Let's say you have a temper with a hair trigger, something that you are aware of and embarrassed by. You've been dealing with it by denying it. You bottle it up as much as possible but sometimes it just explodes and you fly off the handle. Now you avoid situations that might make you angry and because of this you've ended up with few friends and no real social life—which is out of whack with what you really want. So, start stalking, start observing yourself, find out what really makes you angry. Then start confronting it little by little. Begin with a

situation that makes you mildly angry. Let's say someone uses all the milk at work and doesn't replace it. You go to make yourself a coffee and find that there's no milk. You feel the anger well up inside of you until your hand starts to shake on the fridge door. But you do nothing. Usually you'd spend the rest of the day in a foul mood and take it out on everyone else, then feel bad about yourself when you got home. If you do this you are being totally reactive; you're allowing your energy to drain out of you. When you get home you have no personal power left for confronting the things you really want to confront. You have no personal power left to work at changing you.

Instead, just watch yourself, concentrate on your breathing, and allow the emotion to arise. Keep breathing as you look at your anger and see what it is doing to you. Don't hold it in but don't buy into it either—just let it pass. You will find that it gradually subsides to a level where you are back in control. Now, gently and with a smile on your face, go and find out who drank all the milk and beat the shit out of them, errr . . . I mean ask them to go and get some more.

If you do this, you are in control. You will have energy to put into the things you really want, rather than wasting it on things that are not aligned to what you want. The more often you do this with little things, the more capable you will be of confronting big things. Slowly you will rebaptize anger as assertiveness.

You can do the same with any other quality you dislike

in yourself. If you find that you are beating yourself up then do something about it. If you are selfish then watch yourself, monitor the things that you do. Wait for an opportunity, then confront your selfishness and rebaptise it as self-reliance. Then you can help others who aren't able to look after themselves.

When you stop expending energy on suppressing your dark side, you will find you have much more energy for addressing the things you really need to face. Like the fears we discussed in the last chapter . . .

paradigm inertia

have you ever been driving a car to a place you've never been before while someone in the passenger seat with a street map on their lap gives directions? Just as you go through an intersection they say, "Turn right there!" That's paradigm inertia. You overshoot intersections and have to back up to them.

You have energy invested in the way you've been living your life, in the way you've been doing things. That's why it's hard to change. The inertia from your old way of acting can send you hurtling straight through the intersection at which you need to turn.

You're like the *Titanic*—overloaded with small rudders. It takes time to change direction. In the meantime you could go crashing into the icebergs in your path.

DO

how do you deal with this?

Acknowledge it. Accept that it will take time to change direction. Then start working out which things are pushing you in a direction you don't want to go.

In *BE* we talked about the idea that, at any given time, our lives are full. So to make space for something new first you have to let something go.

Well, everything you do has a degree of inertia attached to it. You have to work out which things you need to let go.

I used to live in a shared house with two other people. Between us we had a large group of friends who used to party together. Our house was rather big and had a huge cellar so we all used to get together there. As well as partying on the weekend we also had "Tuesday night" sessions. We'd get together, drink, sing and carry on till the wee hours—there was even a song written about it! As much fun as it was, Tuesday night often meant that for the rest of the week I was a wreck—I was just going through the motions rather than striving to do what I really wanted. Tuesday night had an inertia that kept me going in a direction I didn't want to go. I kept seeing the intersection but I just couldn't turn in time.

Do you have a Tuesday night inertia problem? If so, work out what it is. Get ready to let it go to make space for something new.

These are the things I need to let go so I can make space for something new . . .

_____

_____

_____

_____

_____

_____

_____

_____

_____

_____

_____

_____

NOTES

strategic intent

if you want to achieve your dreams you need to have a strategy. Otherwise everything is just too big, too hard, and too confronting to change.

Think of it as a Monopoly game. When you play Monopoly do you have a strategy? Most people do. Either buy nothing and accumulate cash, or buy everything and hope that enough people land on your real estate and pay you rent before you run out of cash. Some people have a variation where they only buy sets of real estate or only the utilities. The point is, if you have a strategy you have clarity of intent. You know which little steps you need to take along the way. Without a strategy you just flounder from place to place, maybe buying, maybe not.

It's the same when making life changes. If you play the life game according to a strategy you know which little

steps are along the way. You also know what you're trying to achieve.

how do you do this? break it down.

Let's say you decide you want to live in a house by the sea with a vegetable garden. At the moment, you live in a small, inner-city apartment. You need a strategy. Most people in this situation say, "One day when I have enough money I'll buy my house by the sea." In the meantime, they spend their money on new clothes, new cars, and other things that distract them from their unhappiness. Then they sit and wait for a miracle and their dream of a house by the sea is just another unfulfilled wish.

If you want to live by the sea then there are a whole lot of steps along the way.

> The rung of the ladder was never meant to be rest upon but only to hold a man's foot long enough to enable him to put the other somewhat higher.
> —THOMAS HUXLEY

Do you have a vision of the ladder that stretches away in front of you, linking up with your ideal future?

If not, try this. Go off to a quiet space again and stand in your ideal future. Now ask yourself, *What did I do to get*

here? The answer may be illuminating. It will certainly pro-vide a wealth of ideas for you to choose from. Write them down. Then start breaking them down into when.

What's the first step on the ladder? What comes next?

When you have the list, draw the ladder and write each step on the drawing. Stick it up on your wall. Take the first step on the ladder and start doing it.

the power of patience and persistence

Nothing in the world can take the place of persistence:
Talent will not: nothing is more common than unsuccessful
men with great talent. Genius will not: unrewarded genius
is almost a proverb. Education will not: the world is
full of educated derelicts. Persistence and
determination are omnipotent!
—CALVIN COOLIDGE

I was at a dinner function recently where the guest speaker was legendary Australian Rules football coach Kevin Sheedy. His team, Essendon, which had been hailed as the team of the century, had just lost the Grand Final. Over a few glasses of red I took great delight in nagging him about it. Eventually he turned to me and said, "XXXX off and speak to some of those young coaches who have never taken their team to a Grand Final. I've taken my team to eleven Grand

Finals and we didn't win them all but I can tell you one thing: if you keep knocking on the door eventually they're going to let you in!"

Hmmm . . . Put me back in my box, didn't it?

But what he said is so true! To achieve great things takes time and it's easy to give up along the way. The harder thing is to patiently and persistently strive to achieve what you want.

so how do you do that?

Recognize that you can't fight the world. Meditation will help you remain calm. Belief and faith will help you be persistent. Along the way you will face setbacks, but as Paulo Coelho says in his book *The Alchemist*, "Don't die of thirst in sight of the palm trees."

If you are doing what you love and following your passions then the journey will be the destination. But as well as being present in the journey you must not lose sight of the goal. This brings us to opportunity.

moments loaded
with destiny

All of us, whether or not we are warriors,
have a cubic centimeter of chance that pops out
in front of our eyes from time to time. The difference
between an average man and a warrior is that
the warrior is aware of this, and one of his tasks is
to be alert, deliberately waiting, so that when his
cubic centimeter pops out he has the necessary
speed, the prowess, to pick it up.
—CARLOS CASTANEDA

there are many different ways of looking at the world, and we all seek certainty so that we can have peace of mind. In each civilization people collectively decide how they believe the world to be and then they act in a way that constantly reinforces that belief.

Some civilizations believed that the world was flat so

they avoided traveling to its edges lest they fall off. Tribal people in the jungles of South America believe that spirits and gods rule the world, causing good times or bad, so they build shrines and make offerings to them. The Australian Aborigines believe that spirits inhabit some places so there are sacred sites where few are allowed to tread.

In this Western civilization we see time as a linear construct. It can be measured and divided into hours, minutes, and days. We work with time in the same way we work with a slide rule. It reaches back behind us and stretches out in front of us.

But how often have you been in situations where time has seemed to compress and fly past? Or when time seemed to move so slowly you could almost touch it? People who have been in car accidents often describe the way time stood still as they saw what was about to happen.

My point is that we act in accordance with our perceptions. The collective view of a civilization reinforces a particular perception of the world. Even if you knew in your heart that time stood still, your logical mind, reinforced by what you have been led to believe is the truth, would tell you otherwise.

But what if every possible future existed in every possible moment?

What if time, rather than being a singular, linear construct, was a series of interwoven nonlinear paths?

In every moment and with every decision we make, we decide which of those paths to follow. Look back on your

life. What were the critical moments of your life? Where did you make decisions that changed its course? Maybe you decided to leave a long-term relationship. Maybe you quit a corporate job to work for a charity. Maybe you made the decision to stand up for your beliefs and that caused you to change direction in life.

do you see what I mean?

The problem is that sometimes these alternative paths are far apart, leaving you no choice but to stay on the path you are on. This is where paradigm inertia comes in. You are on the train barreling along and can't get off until it slows down to take a corner. But sometimes paths come perilously close together and if you recognize how close they are you can jump across to another possible future. These are the critical moments, the junction points of our lives.

Hold that thought for a moment and imagine that you are a fish swimming down a fast-flowing river. You only eat one particular type of food and you are moving fast so you need to be alert. Because you are alert, you ignore the small grubs and fish that come into your field of vision. Instead, you wait for exactly what you want. You wait patiently until the moment arrives and when it does, you seize the moment and your prey.

Life is like that. A river that takes us very quickly from start to finish. Along the way there are lots of different things

that come into our field but only some of them are worth exploring. If you don't know what you want then you are drawn from one thing to another. Instead of providing you with what you need, these things just provide distraction. They aren't what you need so you get weaker and weaker, which makes you poorer and poorer at finding the food you really need. Slowly you wither away.

But, and yes, this is a big BUT, if you know what you really want and you are patient, then like the fish you will flow along the river of life waiting and waiting until the opportunity arises. When it does, without hesitation you can grasp the moment.

Now combine this with the idea of junction points in time. If you know what you want you can grasp what you need as you go, and this makes you strong and alert. Then you will wait patiently for the critical moment to arise, that junction point to an alternative future. You will see your cubic centimeter of opportunity, and jump!

These are the moments that are loaded with destiny. These are the windows of opportunity that are open for a moment but if you don't jump through they will slam shut in your face. This is why you need to do the work to be prepared and ready.

the pillars

To accomplish great things,
we must not only act,
but also dream;
not only plan,
but also believe.
—ANATOLE FRANCE

we're at the end of the first part of this book. I hope you're finding it useful so far. I know it's a lot of information to take in and if you're a big picture person like me you might appreciate a diagram. I know it's a very "dry" way of looking at things, but sometimes it helps to put things into perspective. If you don't like diagrams ignore page 64, and if you do here's a summary.

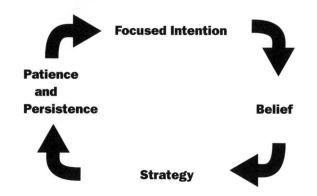

Focused Intention

Patience
and
Persistence

Belief

Strategy

These are the pillars of successful action. Focus your intention, develop belief around it, devise a strategy, then patiently and persistently implement the strategy. Once you see what happens you can go around again—but I'm getting ahead of myself so let's move on to happiness.

where from?

Angels can fly because
they take themselves lightly.
—ANON

we talked a whole lot about happiness in *BE*, so I'm
not going to repeat it here. But I will say that I believe happiness arises from finding the authentic you and then doing
what you really want to do with integrity, so you can be who
you really want to be. If you're living an authentic life then
you're living your passions and you'll be lost in the flow of
life, savoring every moment.

So, the first thing is to LET YOURSELF OFF THE HOOK!

Our dreams and ideals can be things that we joyfully
strive toward or they can become big hooks that we willingly
use to hang ourselves.

A little while ago I returned from Africa to Australia with this great dream of setting up a retreat center where people could take time out to think about all this sort of stuff. I was living in an amazing house right on the beach in far north Queensland. I thought it was the ideal place for the retreat center so I invited a couple of people I knew, who were sound healers, to visit and run some workshops.

Everyone who visited me in that house knew right away that it was paradise. From the house you looked through a few palm trees to the sea and once you were down on the beach there was about one and a quarter miles of almost-private sand to walk along. Mountains rose up behind the house, covered in lush forest. It was like a dream.

The problem was that no one there was the slightest bit interested in doing workshops that required anything that even slightly resembled thinking. People in that neck of the woods wanted to sit on the beach in the sun, swim in the ocean, go out to dinner, get drunk, and generally have a mindlessly good time.

but there i was with my dream . . .

The fact that it wasn't working frustrated the hell out of me and I spent a lot of my time beating myself up about it. Until, bless her soul, as we walked along the beach one

evening at sunset, my friend turned to me and said, "Don't let your dreams hang you. It's okay to let it go. So what if it doesn't work here? It just means you haven't found the right place yet."

Get it? Remember it's a light journey, not a heavy journey. You get to choose through the way you respond to things.

hozho

the principle concept of Navajo metaphysics says we must walk in harmony with the earth and ourselves lest we do damage to both. *Hozho* is the word that describes this balance and it is a key element in being happy.

In our push-push world it's easy to lose balance. We get a big project at work and tell ourselves that just for this week we will work twelve-hour days to get it done. But when it's finished the boss is so pleased he gives us a new project and a big pat on the back. So we keep working long hours and before too long we find there is no time to exercise and only a limited amount of time for seeing friends. But there is work and there is recognition.

don't be lured into the velvet ghetto!

It's a saying I heard in New York. It's a term used by a group of lawyers who work incredibly long hours and get paid

amazing amounts of money. They buy expensive suits, new cars, and apartments, join exclusive clubs and frequent the trendiest restaurants. BUT, they are unhappy . . .

The velvet ghetto lures them in, traps them into a way of life and they don't know how to get out of it.

are you in a velvet ghetto?

There's nothing wrong with nice clothes, expensive cars, or material wealth. The trick is to have balance. You don't have to be poor and eat nothing but mung beans to be happy—whoever said that probably never had any money so came up with a convenient excuse. Likewise, money can't buy you happiness.

Balance in all parts of life—mental, emotional, physical, and spiritual. It's the middle path you need to seek, the balance between logic and emotion, work and play, striving and enjoying.

so how do you do it?

First, make a conscious decision to lead a balanced life. I'll bet that when you did your ideal-you visioning, you didn't see yourself spending all your time at work, never seeing friends.

You need to know when you are out of balance. Once again this is where the observer comes in. Listen to how you are feeling when you take your quiet moments. Don't ignore your feelings; be prepared to act on them.

If all you are doing is striving then make some time to smell the roses.

The Native Americans say that in the West we get things wrong—we receive with the mind, analyze with the spirit, hold with the emotions, and give with the body. They believe this causes imbalance because we limit ourselves to what we can logically understand. Then we try and sense the right course. We hold onto our emotions out of fear and this causes us to block up, and then we try to show our love and affection by giving physical things as gifts.

They say we should open ourselves up and receive with the spirit, so we see all the possibilities. Then we should analyse with the mind, hold with the body, and give with the emotions.

It's a different way of looking at the world, I know, but think about it. It makes sense doesn't it?

If you are in balance then you can be the source.

be the source

The future belongs to those
who believe in the beauty
of their dreams.
—ELEANOR ROOSEVELT

if you want to be happy you can't wait for others to bring happiness to you. Happiness arises from doing what you want to do with integrity and being who you want to be. This means that you have to be the source of your own vision and values. By owning and taking responsibility for your vision and values you can become the source of your own happiness too.

Have you ever dreamed of doing something great, but not been sure if you could do it? Did you go to your family and friends and tell them about your dream, hoping they

would be excited about it and convince you that you could achieve it?

That's not taking ownership of your dream, and that's not taking responsibility for your dream. By doing that you are also vulnerable to those people who are threatened by your dreams—they're the ones who had dreams but compromised and gave up on them. They're the people who will tell you why you can't live your dream and then they try really hard to put you back in your box.

It's easy to get upset when confronted by a situation like this. But look at it the other way around. These people often view the world as a tough place where you can't always get what you want. Then here you are, telling them that you're going out to do something amazing. If they agree with you and support you they invalidate their view of life. They invalidate the actions they've taken in the past that made them give up on their dreams. This would mean admitting they gave up too soon, and that they have failed. So if you seek support for your dreams don't be surprised to find that it provokes an angry response from some people.

You can't expect other people to get excited about your vision unless you are. That's the simple truth and that's why you need to do all the preparatory work. Try on the future and visualize.

If you've done the visualization and addressed your fears you will know how you FEEL about your vision. This is of fundamental importance—feeling is the language of

creation. Our moods are affected by the way we relate to things, and it is here that interaction becomes key.

Let me explain. If you go and hide in a hut somewhere and do all the preparatory work on your vision, you will have a very clear idea of what you want, a clear intent, you will believe in its eventuality and you will be facing your fears. In an isolated environment you are the true source. You will not be confronted by any other view on life but your own.

However, life in our age is not like that. You must interact with others and you must face, and possibly clash with, their views of life. This means that our responses to interaction with others are fundamental to our being.

When you decide to be the source of your vision and values by owning them and taking responsibility for them, an amazing thing happens. Simply through the act of consciously deciding this you change your relationship with the world. You alter your way of being and this makes other things possible.

Instead of being the pinball and bouncing from one view to the next, always in reactive mode, always subject to the influence of others, you become more stable, more secure, more capable of supporting not only your vision but the visions of others as well.

There are some tricks to doing this and we'll look at them in a moment. First, what about the concept of Karma?

captain karma and
the dharma police

As long as you keep a person down, some part of you has to
be down there to hold him down, so it means you cannot
soar as you otherwise might.
—MARIAN ANDERSON

karma is an interesting concept found in
virtually all religious or spiritual teachings. Karma itself
is just the energy attached to an action. The idea is that
whatever energy you put into an action comes back to
you—good or bad. From a Christian perspective it is
captured in the words "As you sow so shall ye reap."
In physics one of the basic laws is that energy cannot be
destroyed. The Buddhists believe that you can accumulate good Karma from lifetime to lifetime, and that more
enlightened beings often choose to come into this world

DO

in a challenging life because it holds greater opportunities for spiritual growth.

So, from a happiness perspective, Karma is fundamental. Karmic loops can have a profound effect on our lives. Consider the person who has given up on their dreams and compromised—settled for a life that does not make them happy. You come along, full of life and excited about your vision. They quickly slap you down and you run off with your tail between your legs. But even though they've told you to pull your head in and stop being so ridiculous, a little part of them will be taken back to the time when they had grand dreams in their heart. A little part of them will be screaming to be heard. Soon, however, as sure as like attracts like, one of their friends will drop in to see them. Your name will come up in conversation, your dream will be discussed. For a moment they will reminisce about the times they had dreams. Then they will pull apart your dream, producing a myriad reasons why it isn't possible. Soon they will have reinforced their shared view of the world as a nasty place where dreams are just that, dreams, and where reality is a chore. Their own dreams are safely back in the bottle. Their view of the world has been reinforced and they can go back to their lives, pretty certain but not quite sure that it is the only way to live.

You, on the other hand, have become the source of your vision and values, and escaped the reactive loop. You will find that you begin to draw toward you people who have the

same view of the world as an abundant place of opportunity where anything is possible. As you change your relationship with the world don't be surprised to find that you see less and less of the people who knock your dreams, and more and more of people who are striving to achieve their dreams. Karma really does go around and the key is to be the source.

The Dharma police are the other ones you've got to watch out for. In Buddhism there are three jewels in which you can take refuge—Buddha, or more specifically the Buddha nature, Dharma, the spiritual teachings, and Sanga, the spiritual community.

I came across the term "Dharma police" at a meditation retreat a few years ago. It was one of those retreats where you have to get up really early and there were lots of rules for what you could and couldn't do. Of course, many people broke the rules, and there were some people at the meditation center who used to check up on participants. They weren't teachers, just people helping out, and they took great delight in catching people out—hence the term "the Dharma police."

I'm bringing it up now because there seems to be a whole lot of Dharma police in every walk of life. They are "holier than thou" and take great delight in catching people out and telling them off the whole time.

Often these are the people who have done just a little bit of work on themselves. Then they decide they know it all

and are ready to "help" others to get their act together. This involves telling others what they are doing wrong and shitting on them from a great height.

do you know someone like that?

I've encountered a whole lot of them in my time and they all suffer from "spiritual pride." They figure that they know best. But what I've worked out over the years is that more often than not it's THEIR issue and NOT yours.

As I said, these people have often done enough searching along a spiritual path to know what they should and shouldn't be doing. But they usually find that there is an aspect of their personality that they can't quite control. This causes anger, and instead of letting themselves off the hook they redirect their anger toward other people and become practicing members of the Dharma police!

Here's an example. Years ago I met a woman who I thought was really together. She had an amazingly powerful energy and would often engage people in long and deep conversations about spiritual matters. After knowing her for a period of time, I discovered there was an aspect of her life that was completely out of control. She was well and truly dependent on having a joint or two at the end of the day in order to cope with her life. Now, even though she wouldn't admit it, her dependency obviously caused her great angst. She dealt with this angst by being the first person to tell you

where, how, and to what degree you needed to do work on yourself. She would destroy all the good stuff she was doing in one moment of anger. People became wary of her and stopped engaging with her. This made her even more aloof and even more dependent on her joint at the end of the day. And so the cycle continued.

are you a card-carrying member of the dharma police?

If you are, then please take a moment to think about the values you are practicing. Compassion is much nicer than judgment. Alternatively, if you are saddled with someone who is constantly on your back about the things you do wrong, then this person is a real challenge to your happiness. The Dharma police are looking for an argument. The first thing you need to do is stop reacting.

bulletproof
positive attitude

everywhere we go, every-
thing we do and everyone we meet has some effect on us.
It can be good, bad or indifferent, but recognize that there
is an effect. Now you can do something about it.

Imagine that the world is full of pure energy. Everything has
energy attached to it and everybody has their own energy.

Now see yourself as a sphere of energy. Everywhere
you go you either pick up or leave energy. You put energy into
everything you do and every time you interact with someone
you exchange energy.

The trick is to know whether this energetic interaction is
good or bad AND how it fits in relation to your context. In
other words, how does it fit in with what you want?

I'm sure you know places that make you feel good and
others that make you feel bad. In order to be happy you

need to find places that make you feel good and avoid places that make you feel bad. If you check in with your observer it is relatively easy to identify which places are good and which are bad. Then you need to take responsibility and do something about it. However, within the context of what you want to do and the steps on your ladder, you may have to spend time in places that make you feel bad, in your journey to the place that makes you feel good.

It's a similar thing with people. I'm sure you interact with some people who leave you feeling drained. They're the ones who come to you and only want to talk about themselves and their dramas. They are energy vultures who literally suck the life out of you.

how do you deal with this?

Well, first, be aware. You need to be in touch with yourself so that you recognize what is happening.

A great thing to do in your morning meditations is to enclose yourself in a bulletproof positive attitude. When you've calmed your mind, imagine that you have a sphere of energy that reaches up above your head, all around you, and down below your feet. Now imagine that your sphere is filling up with white light and then make the outer edge of it bulletproof positive. Set your intention so that nothing

but positive energy can come within your sphere and nothing but positive energy will go out from you into the world.

Now when you go off into the world and meet people who are energy vultures, don't buy into what they are saying and just react to it, check in with your bulletproof positive sphere. What sort of energy are you letting in? What sort of energy are you putting out?

If you find that negative energy is penetrating your sphere then consciously imagine it closing and feel that negative energy just bouncing off. Likewise if you feel yourself directing angry energy toward another person, turn it around. Consciously stop projecting that feeling and recognize that this person is in need. Direct positive energy toward them instead.

You will find that it won't be long until the other person realizes they are not getting the reaction they want from you. They'll probably step up their game to another level, perhaps becoming angry or emotional. They want you to react in the way THEY want so that they can suck some energy from you—DON'T. Remain calm, remain conscious of your energy sphere. Don't confuse their issue with your issue. Allow them to have their say but don't buy into it.

It's the same with places. If you know you have to go to a place that you find draining, be prepared. Be aware of your energy field and don't allow yourself to be drained.

Know this though—it takes a lot of personal power to maintain bulletproof positive energy. Recognize this and

nurture yourself, stalk yourself, and store enough personal power to be capable of this. Balance is the key. Be fit mentally, emotionally, physically, and spiritually. Get serious about fulfilling your dreams, get serious about being the authentic you. Spend the time doing your morning meditation. Spend the time maintaining energy so that you can be the source of your vision and values. Take the time to go to places that restore your energy.

The third area where there are energy issues is with the things you do or have done. We put energy into everything we do. By completing things we allow the energy flow to finish and the "thing" to stand on its own. If things are not complete the energy flow remains open and it becomes a drain on our energy.

Years ago I wrote a novel. It was the first major thing I had written and I thought it was great. I'd put a huge amount of energy and time into it and I really wanted to see it published. I showed it to over twenty publishers and every single one of them said that it was good but needed work. None of them, however, could tell me exactly what sort of work it needed. I was frustrated and depressed so I threw the manuscript to one side and tried to forget about it. But every now and then in a quiet moment I would think about it and it just kept bugging me. The energy flow from me to that manuscript was still open and it was draining me. Finally I recognized this and did some work to turn it into a

screenplay. It's never been made into a film BUT the flow of energy between me and that manuscript was complete. Suddenly I had energy to devote to other projects.

Think about your life. Are there projects you have started but not finished that are constantly nagging at you? Is there an interaction that you've had with someone that's not complete?

Make a list of them and then go and do something about them. Make them complete so that you are not being drained of your precious energy. Then you will have more energy to act on your dreams.

don't blink!

Hold your nerve.
If you're not living on the edge
you're taking up too much space.
—ANON

you've done all the work to get you to the
starting blocks and you're standing on the precipice of your
dreams. Now DON'T BLINK! With your eyes wide open you
need to take a deep breath and jump!

One of the best examples of this is in tennis. Wimbledon
is arguably the pinnacle of tennis and the finals often
become a study not just of skill but of sheer mental determination and grit. How often have you seen an underdog
take on a top seed and get them all the way to three sets

down and match point before the emotion of the moment overwhelms them? The top seed has been there before. They know what it feels like, they delay the moment for as long as possible, they allow the tension to build and build, they fight for every point. The challenger becomes more and more nervous. They start thinking about the victory and what it means, they close their eyes to the moment and bingo, the top seed pounces! The top seed wins the set and the match goes on. Now the challenger thinks only of the lost opportunity. Their eyes are still closed to the moment, they get more and more frustrated, their game goes, and eventually they lose.

Now don't get me wrong here. It's no good being an ice-cold, unfeeling, detached robot. That's not living at all, and we all need to feel. However, you need to distinguish between nervousness and excitement. I took some eight-year-old kids to an amusement park recently. They wanted to go on all of the deadly rides, especially the ones which involved being strapped into some contraption that sent you through endless loop-the-loops and other gravity-defying motions. I was nervous, they were excited. As we waited in line, I was pensive, short of breath, and uncommunicative. They were jumping up and down, swinging on things, pushing each other about, and generally being loud. You know what it made me wonder? Do kids get nervous? I don't think so; I think we learn how to do that. So if we learn how to get

nervous, surely we can learn how not to? Let go of your fear of consequences and drop your nervousness. Be in the moment and embrace excitement.

When faced with a moment that is loaded with destiny you need to be right there in that moment with your eyes wide open. If you're trying to be in the present and the future at the same time, your energy will be split and you will be weaker in the present. Likewise, if you are in the past thinking about what happened last time, then you won't be at full strength in the present. In that split second of the present, the past and the future are irrelevant. There is only now so you need to be here.

You can't see what will happen in the future so why worry about it? You can't change the past so why worry about that?

But what happens if it doesn't turn out the way you want?

don't fight the world

Always keep your balance. Your dreams come true
only when your feet are on the ground. Keep going,
you can never tell when a miracle will occur.
—BILL CLINTON

when things don't go your way it's easy to get
angry at the world, to throw your toys around and refuse to
play anymore. But where will that get you?

The world moves in mysterious ways and we should
never imagine that we can truly comprehend it. BUT we
should never stop trying. So, you need to be open to whatever happens.

Remember, by changing you and deciding to pursue your
dreams, you're diving into a very different pool. You're going
to make ripples and you can't know what effect those

DO

ripples will have and how they will come back to you.

If you're open to whatever happens as a result of your actions then you're able to see the opportunities that arise. Accept that whatever happens is right for you right now. Remember the Past, Present, Future way of looking at the world. There is no right and wrong in the present. Something either is or isn't. It's the way we react to it that categorizes it as right or wrong. It's your choice!

While writing this book I had one of those experiences. When I write I like to hide myself away from the world and have no interruptions so I can be clear about what I'm writing. So, with this book I'd been hiding out in a little hut down by a big dam on a huge property at the base of the Drakensberg mountains in South Africa. It was idyllic, no one disturbed me, the view was amazingly inspirational, and the bird life provided as much distraction as I needed.

But then, in the middle of writing, I was told that the owner was coming down for one night and I'd have to move out. "Ahhhhhh! Damn! This is a disaster!" was my first reaction. "I'll never get this book finished; my plans are in disarray!"

Slowly I calmed down and gathered up my things and moved out for the night. Now aside from the benefit of being able to have dinner, drink some wine, and talk with some great people, the next morning a visitor came to the farm who just happened to offer me a work opportunity that I'd been seeking for quite some time!

So, don't imagine that you know better than the universe. Accept whatever is right in front of you and keep your eyes wide open because you never know what amazing things will happen next!

stop, think, then act!

It is not the strongest of the species that survives
nor the most intelligent; it is the one
that is most adaptable to change.
—CHARLES DARWIN

to be able to accept what happens we have to be flexible, but we are all still seeking certainty. Change often provokes an angry response from us. We need to develop a strategy for dealing with change that doesn't derail our grand plans.

I love to go scuba diving. It's a sport which has the mantra, "Stop, think, then act." In scuba diving, if you find yourself in a tricky situation and you panic, you could cause yourself a terrible injury, possibly a fatal one.

When you learn to scuba dive you learn lots of theory but you also practice emergency procedures and rescue drills.

DO

Everyone who dives knows these drills but some people forget the magic ingredient—"Stop, think, then act." It's critical to your survival and often to the survival of others.

There are many examples of this in scuba diving, but let's look at one. Some divers were near a reef which sheltered them from the ocean swells. They had been underwater for some time and became so distracted by the fish life that they lost their way, finding themselves in the ocean currents, too close to the reef to safely surface. One diver began to panic. He tried to swim against the current, but the more he tried the more exhausted he became and the more air he used. Eventually he ran out of air and panicked again. He shot up to the surface and suffered the bends. The other divers had realized they couldn't fight the sea. They remained calm and allowed the current to take them further out into the ocean. As they passed the reef, the current settled down, allowing them to come to the surface and signal the boat with their emergency equipment.

Life's the same. It's not the situation that kills you, it's how you react to it.

The next time you find yourself in a tricky situation, don't panic. Remain calm and maintain focus. Stop, think, then ACT! By acknowledging that the world is constantly changing and accepting whatever happens you give yourself the opportunity to adjust your strategy and adapt to change.

i believe, you believe, we disagree!

Faced with crisis,
the man of character
falls back on himself.
—CHARLES DE GAULLE

values reside in the future as ideals to which we aspire. For instance, most of us would say that we aspire to be truthful in our lives, but few of us can say that we have never told even a white lie. Values clashes provide us with the opportunity to test our values and decide how strongly we believe in them. A value is not a value unless you are willing to sacrifice something to uphold it.

Because our values are so close to our core they also provide great opportunities for bitter and irreconcilable clashes with others. If you take the time to speak with

people who have broken long-term friendships or close relationships you will generally find that at the heart of the matter was a values clash.

If you believe in the value of equality and then discover that one of your oldest friends is racist, you will have trouble resolving the dispute—unless you convince them to change their beliefs or you consciously decide to shelve your beliefs for the sake of the friendship.

The biggest problem with values clashes is that it is difficult to dig down to the heart of the matter, to calmly and definitively determine what is distressing us so much. Sometimes it takes years to really work out what went wrong. By then, of course, it is too late.

But if you take the time to work out exactly what is important in your life and what values you believe in, then you are in a position to take possession of those values and to live authentically.

Values are the building blocks for our personal code of ethics. When faced with an ethical dilemma, try using this model.

First, what is the background to the issue at hand? Has this been going on for some time? Are there any salient issues you need to take into consideration? Are there any other people involved? What is at stake here? A friendship, a close relationship, a business deal?

Now make an estimation of what your options are. You can use three questions to stimulate answers here: What is right? That is, what would be the right thing to do based solely on principle?

What is good? In other words, be a bit Machiavellian here and ask yourself what would be a good outcome. For instance, you may be talking about a long-term friendship. If you take a stand purely on principle it may mean never seeing the person again. But if you are both part of a close group of friends, in reality that would be an untenable position. A good outcome would be that you resolve your differences and remain friends.

The third question is: What is culturally fitting? If you're a Native American and someone has done you wrong, a cul-

turally fitting thing to do might be to spear them in the butt but that may not go down too well in Western society!

Now, list all the possibilities. Try not to eliminate any at this stage, just concentrate on generating them.

Once you have done that, consider the impact of each possibility and eliminate the totally unacceptable ones. Will someone get hurt? (That probably rules out the ever-so-appealing but culturally unacceptable option of spearing the bastard in the butt!) Or will there be a price to pay if it is a business dealing? Is there a time impact? For example, an option may be to kick the person out if you are living with them. (Maybe you could use the spear to prod them out the door if they don't want to go!)

Next, you need to roll out your personal values list and go through and evaluate each possibility.

Finally, make a decision. Remember that an ethical decision is one that you can justify and recommend. In other words, when someone asks you why you made the decision you did, you can say, "I made it because I believe in the value of loyalty and in the same situation I recommend that you do exactly the same." AND you need to be able to live with the decision!

Let's consider an example to see how tricky this can get.

Imagine you are at college and have just completed your exams but don't know the results yet. A good friend of yours is a computer whiz. He tells you he's managed to hack into the mainframe computer and then tells you what your

results are. Your grades aren't good enough to get you into the postgraduate course you've been working toward for four years, but your friend says he can change your grades without anybody ever finding out.

The background. You've always dreamed of getting into a certain prestigious university and you need just one more credit point to get in. You know that one of the lecturers dislikes you intensely and you've suspected all along that they've been giving you poor grades based on your personality rather than your work. You also know that the situation is the opposite with several young girls who've been sucking up to the lecturer all year long. You've also been friends with the computer whiz for many years and you know he'd never tell a soul if you went ahead with it.

Estimate and list. The right thing to do would be to do nothing. A good outcome would be that you get into the university you want and nobody is the wiser. A fitting outcome, based on the dubious grading methods of the lecturer in question, would be for you to get the grade you deserve.

Eliminate the unacceptable. In all of these options no one would suffer bodily harm, and assuming that no one would find out, there are no real repercussions.

Values. The values in question here are honesty and fairness. It would be dishonest to change the results. But then the lecturer has been unfair in the way he has been grading, so surely that justifies changing the grades?

The decision. Well, that's just the point, isn't it? You could take either option and justify the decision, but I imagine that for most people there is only one decision that you could live with.

The point is that if you decide to do nothing and uphold the value of honesty you pay the price by missing out on the university you want. BUT your integrity will still be intact.

Now the twist. Your friend goes ahead and changes his grades anyway, gets into the university you wanted to get into, and then tells you what an idiot you are for not going along with him. Where's that spear now?

A week later you and your friend are called into the dean's office. The dean looks at you both and says that there have been some serious irregularities with the results given. Do you have anything to say?

You never know what's going to happen next, remember? So from the perspective of happiness, you need to be clear about your values and then be willing to live by them. If you decide to live an authentic life then there is a payoff but there's also a price.

stay in the conversation

recently some friends of mine experienced a values clash similar to the example in the last section. For the purpose of this story, let's call them Belinda and Duncan. The dispute arose over a business deal. Both sides thought they were right and vigorously opposed the stance taken by the other. When I found out about it several weeks later they weren't even talking to each other. It had reached the stage where each side was rallying support for their view of the situation. In their eyes you were either for them or against them—there was no middle ground.

To me it was a bizarre situation. They had been good friends the last time I'd seen them, excited about their new business venture. To see the situation deteriorate into open hostility was distressing, especially when all they

wanted to talk about was how they were right and the other person was wrong.

Eventually Belinda calmed down enough to explain that what made her really angry was the fact that Duncan didn't want to talk to her about it. All she really wanted was to have a "vigorous conversation" with him and thrash things out. What had really infuriated her was the judgment that had been made on her character and the lack of opportunity to "appeal" the decision.

It turned out that Duncan, who was a much quieter character, was afraid of discussing the situation face to face because he was intimidated by Belinda's more direct nature.

A Mexican standoff to be sure—but how to get out of it? There's a whole range of issues in situations like this, but I've found the most important questions to ask are: *What do you want and what are you willing to do to get it? What's your commitment?*

Thinking about these questions gives a really different perspective to the normal reactiveness of who's right and who's wrong. It also requires a willingness to let go of judgement and embrace the possibility of forgiveness. Not just for the other person—that's the easy part—but for yourself!

Let me explain. I had been living in the country and had to come back to the city for a work commitment. I needed somewhere to stay and I really didn't want to live on my own. I asked around and a friend of mine suggested staying with

another friend who had a large house with a couple of spare rooms. Anyway, I went and stayed in this beautiful house with a swimming pool and all the latest modern conveniences—life was rosy.

After a few months I started to feel that my time was up, that I'd better leave lest I outstay my welcome. You know that point I mean? When you start to cross over from being a guest to being a resident and relationships start to change? When people start asking you where you are going next and you start wondering the same thing? When the little things bug you that never did when you were just a guest—like what sort of milk is in the fridge, what show is on the television, and why the bottles aren't being put in the recycling bin?

Anyway, I decided it was time to go and sat my friend down to tell him this, figuring he'd been thinking the same thing. That he'd be relieved he didn't have to tell me to get the hell out of his house. But here's where he showed me just how enlightened he is. I thought he'd say, "Okay, well, it will be a shame to see you go," all the while thinking, "Thank God! I don't have to tell the silly bugger to go, he's finally getting his act together." Instead he said to me, "Well, if you feel you have to leave then go right ahead. But the real challenge to our friendship would be if you stayed and we get to the stage where we get on each other's nerves, have nowhere to run, and have to work through it instead. That's where the real opportunity is to take things to a new level."

DO

Ohhh? Okay. What a wake-up call!

It's never the other person we are afraid of—it's ourselves! As people get really close to us they act as a mirror for our imperfections and we revile against ourselves. The true challenge is to have the courage to stay in the conversation and work through the issues, allowing ourselves to see an accurate reflection in truth.

Again, I'm not saying this is easy. But if you can find the courage to stay in the conversation rather than walking away, then natural resolutions to conflict will arise, resolutions that are built on truth and compassion rather than judgment and anger. The beauty of these solutions is that they allow for completion and enable you to move on. But— yes, there's always a but, isn't there?—it means you have to let go of being right all the time . . .

learning to fly

For love to speak true to power,
it must prove its freedom of all fear.
—*The Needs of Strangers*, MICHAEL IGNATIEF

letting go of your notion of control can be a very challenging thing. Being open to whatever happens and accepting it joyfully without fighting the world is very difficult . . . unless you reprogram your brain to have an abundance mentality rather than a scarcity mentality.

To a scarcity mentality the world has only limited possibilities. To an abundance mentality, the world is full of endless possibilities. From a scarcity perspective, your friend who hacked into the computer and changed his grades has YOUR place at the university YOU wanted to get into. Will you resent your friend forever, decide that he's wrong and you're right, and begin lobbying your mutual friends to take your side?

From a scarcity perspective, he deserves to be punished. From an abundance perspective, there is more than enough to go around. From an abundance perspective, other opportunities will open up. If you stop fighting the world then maybe, just maybe, that university was not the right one for you.

Stop worrying about what other people are getting. Start realizing that just because someone else gets something doesn't mean that there isn't something for you, too. Remember, it's their issue not yours.

How do you do this? Remember Captain Karma? Let go of your fear that you will miss out and start giving instead. Start putting into the world what you would like to get out of the world.

gratitude
takes you to joy

there is good in EVERY situation, it's just that sometimes it can take a little while to find it. There can be no joy without gratitude. If you take on a scarcity mentality, resenting other people for what they have and becoming angry at what you get, then you will only cause yourself unhappiness.

In every situation, no matter how bad, ask yourself this: *What is good about this situation?*

Even the worst situations have a silver lining. You can either spend your limited energy fighting the world or you can accept the situation in front of you and focus on the positives.

Relationship breakdowns often make people bitter and twisted. When two people split up after being in a close relationship there is often hurt and anger. This is usually caused

by a fundamental values clash. More often than not, they will both lobby their mutual friends to adopt their version of events. Have you ever been caught in the middle of a situation like this?

How much energy do they spend in trying to convince others that their view is right and the other's is wrong? How often do they say in the middle of their ranting, "I never really loved them anyway!"?

Have you ever had the courage to reply, "Well, what are you complaining about, then? Just get on with your life!"

If you stop and look for the positives in every situation then life can take on a whole new meaning. The key is to take the time in the morning while meditating to remember to be grateful for everything you have. If you do this then you will be able to find joy in your life. In turn you will put out joy into the world, therefore attracting more joy to you.

If you remain bitter, all you do is pee in the collective pool, and nobody likes a pee-er!

here's to the problems of freedom!

when you stop reacting to the world and poke your head up out of the thick pea soup that makes up the dross of reactive life, you'll find an amazing thing—freedom!

Freedom arises from breaking free of the limitations that you've imposed on yourself. Freedom comes from stopping yourself from buying into everyone else's shit. Freedom comes from releasing yourself of expectation and embracing whatever is right in front of you.

Most people never get this far. Most people allow themselves to be seduced into the way of life that society expects of them. Get a good education, get a job, get married, have kids, then wait for your turn in the sun . . .

But some people fight their way out of that. They find their authentic selves and embrace their freedom. Hopefully, that's you! If it is, you are now faced with the problems of freedom.

Do you turn your back on the people in the world who are struggling with their own issues? Or do you engage and take responsibility for changing the world?

No one can make that choice except you. But personally I hope you decide to engage because their freedom IS your freedom . . .

DO ONE

the rational fool

> The heart has its reasons
> which reason does not understand.
> —Blaise Pascal

unless you decide to become a hermit and go and live in a little hut in the mountains, you will have to interact with other people. The rational fool is the person who makes short-term decisions for their own benefit, failing to consider the effects their actions have on others.

Imagine you live in a tribe in remote Africa. To eat you must go out and hunt for your food. If you catch something, rationally, you should eat all of it yourself so that you are strong and have more energy to hunt. But you don't always catch something. So if everyone acted rationally then sometimes you would be nourished and sometimes

you would starve. Everyone would only look after themselves and the tribe as a whole would be weak. However, if you share your catch with everyone else then they will share with you and you will all eat on a regular basis. The rational person is a fool because in the long term they cut their own throat.

Now, bring it into our world. The rational fool is the person who only looks after themselves. They always take more than their share of food at dinner parties, they bring a couple of cheap beers to a party, then drink other people's expensive beer because they know they won't get caught, they cheat on their golf scorecards, they backstab people at work for their own benefit, they cut in when there's a line of people waiting, they take advantage of your generosity but never return the favor. Know what I mean?

In the short term these people benefit, but in the long term they generally get caught out. People collectively decide that they are assholes and choose to avoid them. Usually by this stage the rational fool has moved on to other pastures.

what is the antidote to the rational fool? reputation.

Rationally, we should never form long-term relationships with others because the longer the relationship the more

open we are to being hurt in some way. This applies to both personal relationships and business relationships. The breakdown of a relationship after one month is nowhere near as tragic and hurtful as a breakdown after twenty years.

We get around our limiting rationality through our emotions. Love and shared passions attract us to forming bonds with others. Aside from the obvious benefits, guilt, honor, compassion, and shame stop us from "fleeing to the self" and breaking the commitments we have made when better "rational" options arise.

Our emotions allow us to override our rational thoughts and fears and get more from life by forging reciprocal and mutually beneficial relationships. As emotional beings we look for these relationships all the time. Generally we are willing to give others the benefit of the doubt (or enough rope to hang themselves if you are a cynic . . .) so that we can begin a reciprocal relationship.

When beginning a relationship we watch the other person's actions. We reflect on whether the way they are being is in line with what they say they believe AND whether or not this matches our beliefs. If we approve, we grant them more trust and begin to form a trust spiral. The longer it goes on with no breaches, the more and more we trust them. This is why the breakdown of long-term relationships is so much more painful—the bonds of trust are much deeper, we have revealed far more of ourselves to them.

Your reputation is key because it generally precedes you, determining how much benefit of the doubt people will give you.

If you decide you don't want to form relationships with people (possibly because you have been hurt in the past), then the only person you deceive and hinder is yourself. You are being a rational fool.

the big puzzle

Each lifetime is the pieces of a jigsaw puzzle.
For some there are more pieces. For others the puzzle
is more difficult to assemble. But know this:
you do not have within yourself all of the pieces
of your puzzle. Everyone carries with them at least one
and possibly many pieces to someone else's puzzle . . .
When you present your piece, which is worthless to you,
to another, whether you know it or not,
you are a messenger from the most High.
—RABBI LAWRENCE KUSHNER

if you're the type of person who figures that you can work out all your stuff on your own and not be reliant on other people at all, then now it's your turn to say, "Damn!"

Whoever or whatever engineered the grand plan to put us on this earth was very clever. We are interdependent on

one another. If we seek to avoid interaction because of the pain and suffering that has happened in our lives, then we deny ourselves the possibility of being complete.

From an authentic being perspective, our inter-dependency means that—like it or not—you do not only participate in your own future. You also participate in the future manifestation of your community, your generation, and your group of friends.

Let's look at it from the Past, Present, Future perspective.

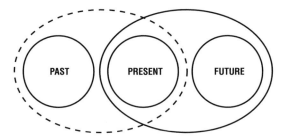

Remember, as an authentic being you take possession and ownership of your future possibilities and then you do some-thing about them in the present. By clarifying your intent, being clear on your beliefs and then acting, you bring your ideal into being.

BUT, while you are doing all this work, others are con-sciously or unconsciously doing the same thing. Many are living inauthentic lives and have relinquished their future possibilities. Some have taken up the challenge and are

actively manifesting good things. Unfortunately there are others who are actively manifesting fear, hatred, anger, and death. If you take all of the manifestations of all of the people on the earth and add them together then you'll get the collective manifestation of all beings. This is what makes our world.

I mentioned that freedom has its own problems. Well, this is one of those problems. What type of world do you want to contribute to?

If you look at all of your friends, some are striving to lead authentic lives and some are still drowning in the quagmire of their fears. How can you participate?

freedom reigns
in truth

There is no God higher than truth.
—MAHATMA GANDHI

an authentic relationship with others is one that assists them in gaining their freedom and allows them to own the unique possibilities for their future. As you go further down the path of authenticity, doing more work to stop the world and your reactions to it, you will find you have more and more energy, or personal power, to assist others.

You can be a mirror for others that will allow them to break out of their own reactiveness and be free. BUT you can only do this through truth. As we discussed in *BE*, the greatest gift you can give others is your whole self in truth. The problem is that a big part of us wants to be

loved by others. This part is fearful of creating upset and hurt, so often avoids or conceals the truth.

To have authentic relationships with others you must place a higher value on truth than on your own comfort.

This is difficult to do in a loving and compassionate way. But by saying no to inauthentic relationships you make room for authentic ones. You will also find that when you get rid of the inauthentic relationships in your life, you will have more energy—the energy-draining relationships will be gone.

So how do you have relationships with others that allow them to own their freedom?

First, you need to acknowledge the temporal nature of existence. By this I mean that everything changes; nothing stands still. We are rolling along through time regardless of what happens. Nothing remains constant. What is the present but a mere flicker between the future and the past? It is here one moment and gone the next. If you recognize this, then movement becomes all-important and the way you flow with the world is key.

The Present is the only place where spirit and matter meet. It is the only place where you have an opportunity to interact with the material world and influence it. It is your point of power. But people get stuck in the loop that goes around and around and around from the Past to the Present and back again. In an authentic relationship with others you need to help them to take responsibility for their future and ACT!

So now you are an incredibly aware and enlightened being. In the next conversation you have with a friend who is struggling with all this stuff, just before you open your big mouth, ask yourself this question: *Is what I am about to say going to give the other person a new opportunity to ACT?*

If the answer is no, keep your big trap shut and think again!

the light at the edge of the world

My humanity is bound up in yours,
for we can only be human together.
—Archbishop Desmond Tutu

when faced with new and challenging situations it's easy to retreat to the self. We all do it at some time. The question is when?

When we are in a comfortable and familiar situation it's easy to be generous and giving. But then take away certainty, take away comfort, make things a little more difficult and you'll find you are soon reduced to survival mode.

The thing is, we are only alone in the world if we believe that we are. If you let go of fear and engage with people you will soon realize that the light at the edge of the world IS people.

DO

You can go to the most amazing, stunningly beautiful places in the world and they will be nothing without people. But people can also make unbearable places a lot more friendly.

I recently found myself in Barcelona, sitting in the marina watching an amazing sunset. As the sun disappeared behind the hills that surround the city, the whole sky turned shades of pink, then orange, and then as if by magic the lights of the city began to appear. It was breathtaking, but all I wanted to do was share it with someone, just to say, "Wow, look at that!"

If you recognize the innate need to connect with others you are halfway towards doing it. But doing it means engaging with others. That can mean revealing ourselves and opening ourselves to the pain of rejection.

If you run from others, in reality you only run from yourself. How do you get over this?

faith and expectation

We must become the change
we wish to see in the world.
—MAHATMA GANDHI

in *BE* we talked a lot about the ideas of unity and oneness. If you look at it from the perspective of faith in human nature it becomes a question of belief and manifestation.

If you have faith in human nature and embrace the idea of unity you expect good people to be around and you manifest this by contributing to good. Remember, we manifest what we intend and what we believe to be the truth. As part of the whole, we play a role in influencing the environment around us.

DO

What do you intend to manifest? What does your ideal world look like? Are your actions aligned to creating this?

I've tried this out many times and I know it is true. Recently I flew into Washington, D.C. When I arrived I was tired and jet-lagged and had little energy for organizing myself. I knew where I was staying and I knew that there was a bus which went to the city but I had no idea where I was supposed to catch it. As the plane taxied in I told myself to have faith in human nature, to trust that because I needed help someone would come to me.

Well, I picked up my bags and started walking out of the terminal. When I reached the pavement I put down my bag and stood there looking around. Sure enough, as I scanned the scene, staring right back at me was a lovely African-American woman with a big smile on her face.

"Are you okay there, honey?" she asked me.

Well, who could not smile back? She told me exactly where to catch my bus and exactly how much it was going to cost me.

This reinforced to me the fact that there are good people in the world wherever you go. If you have faith in human nature they come to you. The trick is, of course, to make sure it's working in reverse. Remember Captain Karma? When you are in your home city and rushing from place to place in your busy life and someone asks you for help, do you take the time to stop and help them?

If not, think about what you are putting into the world. Think about how you can change your way of being so that you ARE the change you wish to see in the world. Don't wait for others to show you proof that people are innately good. Be the one who provides the evidence for others.

i to we

The whole world is you,
yet you keep thinking
there is something else.
—Chinese proverb

maybe you've had a hard life where people have constantly acted in a way that's proved to you that the majority of people are assholes. Maybe you've decided along the way that you'll be wary of people, retreat into your hideout, and look after number one?

If you've been like that but now you see the need to change you're probably wondering how to go about it. The first thing to do is change your perception of your place in the world.

Go back to your quiet space. Calm your mind and see yourself as that sphere of white-light energy. Now, slowly but surely, see your sphere of energy increase in size, expanding out in every direction. As it expands change your viewpoint so that you are rising up like a helicopter. See your place in the geographic world and see your sphere getting bigger and bigger, taking in the region that you are in, then the country, then expanding until it encompasses the entire world.

Now your energy sphere is part of the entire world and you are part of the entire world. Just let it sit like that. Concentrate on your breathing and allow yourself to feel what it is like to be the world. Don't see yourself as being separate to the world, as if you were a spaceman looking down on it. See yourself as part of the world with your energy stretching out in every direction to all places of the world. See yourself as an integral part of the world and see all of the world—the people, the animals, all other life—as part of you.

When you feel comfortable, start projecting positive energy into the world. Wish all beings to be happy, wish all beings to have love and compassion. Put the exact energy into the world that you would like to see in the world. Be part of the solution, not part of the problem.

After a while you will feel a sense of responsibility and joy.

In time, allow your energy sphere to return to its normal size. Finish by setting your intention to have a bulletproof positive attitude.

Now when you meet people during the day, don't see them as being separate to you and possibly some sort of threat. Remember the feeling of oneness from your meditation. See people as being a part of you and you as being a part of them. When you see people as part of you and as part of the interlinked whole, you will treat them completely differently. Instead of telling them what they are doing wrong and getting upset with them, maybe you will try to help them.

Think about it like this. If your big toe was giving you pain would you take a hammer out and start smashing it, yelling at it to behave? Unless you're a masochist, I don't think so. Instead, you try to find out what's wrong and then you try to make it better. You know that you and your toe are interlinked, that your toe's pain is your pain.

It's the same thing here. If you see others as part of an interlinked whole then you can begin to see that their happiness is your happiness. Their freedom is your freedom. There is no separation. To believe otherwise is to be delusional.

Before every meeting and every interaction with people, set your intention to be a positive influence on all those with whom you come into contact. Instead of listening only to what you want to hear, stop focusing on yourself and take the time to really listen to what the person is saying. Take the time to listen to what your little observer tells you that this person is really wanting to communicate to you.

If you can do this you will find that people seek you out and appreciate talking to you and that people will begin to really listen to you. Remember, you must be the change you wish to see in the world.

judgement locks
the gate to possibility

Always leave the cage door open
so the bird can return.
—Chinese proverb

you may be thinking at this point that from now on everyone you meet is going to be nice, caring, and enlightened. Well, sorry to rain on your parade but you're still going to have to deal with the odd asshole or two.

When faced with a nasty, self-centered, uncaring person who goes around spraying negative vibes into the world it's easy to go straight into judgement and damn them for all eternity. But judgment locks the gate to possibility.

Remember the Past, Present, Future thing? And the whole idea of seeing the world as temporal in nature? Well, if you cast judgment upon someone you confine them to the

Past. You prevent them from changing and taking on their future possibilities. You limit them to exactly who they are now rather than who they could be.

Instead if you believe in the highest possibility for all beings and have a clear vision of the future we can create together, you leave open the possibility for them to change.

Remember, just by interacting with people you participate in their being. Every interaction involves an energy exchange, every interaction can be good or bad, and every interaction will have an effect on both you and the other person. The way you choose to interact is fundamental to the world we can create together.

Intention and belief are once again critical to the outcome. You need to plant the seeds of possibility and water them often.

the true impact
of unity

if you don't believe we are interconnected as part of the whole then you will have no reason to try to change the world. You simply won't believe that your little efforts will have any impact.

BUT, if you embrace the notion of interconnectedness and unity then you will see that even the most trivial of your actions can affect everything. Think about that for a second . . .

If we are truly interconnected then just by thinking about the world, having positive intent, and putting it out there, you can influence the world that we create together.

The power of our oneness allows just a few individuals to affect the quality of life of the entire population of the world.

To lift our eyes to heaven when the eyes of others
are on the ground is not easy. To worship at the feet
of angels when others worship fame and riches
is not easy. But perhaps the most difficult of all
is to think the thoughts of the angels,
to speak the words of the angels,
and to do as the angels do.
—*The Isaiah Effect*, GREGG BRADEN

putting it all together

well, here we are at the end of this book so let's put it all together. I believe that if you're going to be happy and fulfilled in life then you must first be able to find the authentic "You." To do that you have to:

- Be serious and committed. Put your ass on the line and be willing to risk who you are now to find the real you.

- Tap into and listen to your observer.

- Be prepared to play with outrageous possibilities and try the future on for size by using visualization meditation.

- Charge your vision with the energy of intention and believe in its inevitability.

- Identify your fears and face them with the courage of a spiritual warrior.

- Acknowledge paradigm inertia and its effects.

- Have a strategy, be patient and persistent, and seize your cubic centimeter of opportunity when it arises.

Once you're on the path of actively striving to live an authentic life then not only will amazing opportunities arise in your path; there will also be challenges to face along the way. In order to be strong and face these situations with courage, one of the biggest things to remember is that YOU CHOSE THIS PATH. You are no longer a victim of circumstance. You are a proactive creator of your world. So you must remain focused, take responsibility, and:

- Let yourself off the hook, don't beat yourself up, and stay balanced along the journey.

- Take ownership and responsibility for your vision and ideals and be the source.

- Have a bulletproof positive attitude, create your own Karma, and don't buy into other people's shit.

- On the precipice of your dreams, don't blink! Hold your eyes wide open, be in the present moment, and act!

- The world moves in mysterious ways so don't fight it, EMBRACE IT!

- In crisis situations, remain calm, maintain focus. Stop, think, then ACT!

- Know what you stand for and be willing to pay the price necessary to uphold your values.

- Remember to be grateful in every situation and embrace the problems of freedom.

The last part of the journey is to be able to transcend the self and be one with all things. This is both the greatest challenge and the most rewarding place to get to, for it can only be reached when one is truly at peace with oneself. It is the stage where miraculous things start to happen because finally you become free of the shackles of the self and the ever present focus of "I." When you find yourself at this stage of the journey, remember:

- Don't be a rational fool.

- Engage with others so that you can complete your life puzzle and help them complete theirs.

- Place a higher value on truth than on your own comfort.

- Have faith in human nature and manifest it.

- Let go of judgment and leave the cage door open.

- Be the change you wish to see in the world!

So, there's a summary of this book but I can't leave without adding that none of this means anything if it just remains an intellectual construct. It's not enough to understand all of these things and to be able to discuss and debate these ideas and concepts with others. Life moves along at a great pace and we are constantly faced with situations where we must fall back on our instinctive responses. It's then that we get to see the real "self," when there is no time to "take a moment" and think about what an appropriate response might be. No amount of intellectualizing will help us then.

So, we must dip our toes into the water and hone our skills, always accepting the result and always striving to be our best in free-flow not just in think-flow. For,

> To know and not to act is yet to know.
> —*The Sea of Tranquillity*, YUKIO MISHIMA

the meaning of life

I know I said there was no easy answer and I do believe that all of us need to make sense of the world in our own way. But years ago I was at a party where we were all invited to write down our version of the meaning of life. So here's mine:

The meaning of life is a deep-seated spiritual challenge that paradoxically we set for ourselves before we choose to enter this unnatural physical world. Once here, blinded by our many delusions, we must face the temptations that go hand in hand with our physical manifestation, bereft of the knowledge of our true nature. This is the meaning of life and this is the test of life. To see if in our blindness we can call on the knowledge rooted in our soul and rise to the challenge. So that when we return to the place we started from, we can look ourselves in the mirror and rejoice!

DO

Looking back on this now I realize that there is one thing that I'd like to add to it. Success is a word that is used often in our linear, outcome-focused Western society. It's something that can really mess with your head because of the way our materialist society defines it. How many times do you get asked: *Are you successful?* When all the inquirer really wants to know is: *How much money do you make?* People want to judge others against a yardstick to see how they are going in a comparative sense. The easiest and seemingly most definitive measure is money. So, how about we change the yardstick?

> To leave the world a bit better
> Whether by a healthy child, a garden patch
> Or a redeemed social condition
> To know even one life has breathed easier
> Because you lived,
> This is to have succeeded.
> —RALPH WALDO EMERSON

My hope is that you can find your true authentic self, live a life that is full of love and joy, and play a part in creating a better world. So it's time now to close this book and go and DO! I wish you well on your journey and I thank you for being part of mine.